LEARN TO WRITE

CURSIVE

Joining Cursive Letters

Tracing & Writing Cursive Letters, States, Capitals, and U.S. Presidents

Guided Cursive Alphabet

Aa Bb Cc Dd

Ee Ff Gg Hh Ii

Jj Kk Ll Mm

Nn Oo Pp Qq Rr

Ss Tt Uu Vv Ww

Xx Yy Zz

Preparing to Write

Position of Arm, Hand, and Pencil.

The full weight of the arm should rest upon the cushion of the muscle in the front of the elbow, thus forming the center of motion and control. The clothing of the forearm should be loose and light, in order to give freedom and ease of movement.

The hand should rest and glide upon the little finger along the side and just back of the nail. This gliding rest should move

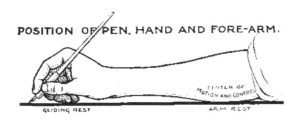

POSITION OF PEN, HAND AND FORE-ARM.

freely toward the right in making the upward strokes in lowercase letters. It should slip freely in large forms such as capitals and long loops.

The pencil should point above and somewhere between the elbow and shoulder. It should cross the hand somewhere near the knuckle joint of the first finger. The pencil should be held at an angle of about forty-five degrees--- the pencil writes most effectively when held at that angle.

The side of the palm of the hand should not touch or rest on the paper, but be kept free, allowing the little finger only to rest in the center of the paper.

The wrist doesn't have to be held flat, it should be allowed to turn far enough to throw the pencil out from the elbow.

The student should hold the pencil firmly without pinching or gripping it. The position should be natural rather than rigid.

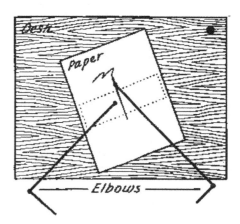

Position or Angle of Paper

The paper should be held close to the body when writing at the top of the sheet, and well from the body when writing near the bottom.

The paper should be held neither parallel with the desk nor at right angles with the forearm, but about midway between these two extremes.

The elbow should be shifted from two to four times in writing across the page, but never when the pencil is on the paper and in motion. Move the elbow between words.

Both elbows should be kept near to the edge of the desk, and be bent at about right angles. The forearm should cross the desk at about forty-five degrees.

Trace the letter Aa. Then write the letter Aa as many times as possible.

$\mathcal{A}$ a

$\mathcal{A}$ $\mathcal{A}$ $\mathcal{A}$

$\mathcal{A}$ $\mathcal{A}$ $\mathcal{A}$

$\mathcal{A}$ $\mathcal{A}$ $\mathcal{A}$

$\mathcal{A}$ $\mathcal{A}$ $\mathcal{A}$

$\mathcal{A}$ $\mathcal{A}$ $\mathcal{A}$

$\mathcal{A}$ $\mathcal{A}$ $\mathcal{A}$

a a a

a a a

a a a

a a a

a a a

Learn to Write in Cursive: Joining Cursive Letters

Trace the letter Bb. Then write the letter Bb as many times as possible.

B *b*

B *B* *B*

B *B* *B*

B *B* *B*

B *B* *B*

B *B* *B*

B *B* *B*

b *b* *b*

b *b* *b*

b *b* *b*

b *b* *b*

b *b* *b*

Trace the letter Cc. Then write the letter Cc as many times as possible.

C c

C C C

C C C

C C C

C C C

C C C

c c c

c c c

c c c

c c c

c c c

Learn to Write in Cursive: Joining Cursive Letters

Trace the letter Dd. Then write the letter Dd as many times as possible.

𝒟 d

𝒟 𝒟 𝒟

𝒟 𝒟 𝒟

𝒟 𝒟 𝒟

𝒟 𝒟 𝒟

𝒟 𝒟 𝒟

𝒟 𝒟 𝒟

d d d

d d d

d d d

d d d

d d d

Trace the letter Ee. Then write the letter Ee as many times as possible.

Learn to Write in Cursive: Joining Cursive Letters

Trace the letter Ff. Then write the letter Ff as many times as possible.

Trace the letter Gg. Then write the letter Gg as many times as possible.

Learn to Write in Cursive: Joining Cursive Letters

Trace the letter Hh. Then write the letter Hh as many times as possible.

Trace the letter Ii. Then write the letter Ii as many times as possible.

Learn to Write in Cursive: Joining Cursive Letters

Trace the letter Jj. Then write the letter Jj as many times as possible.

Trace the letter Kk. Then write the letter Kk as many times as possible.

Learn to Write in Cursive: Joining Cursive Letters

Trace the letter Ll. Then write the letter Ll as many times as possible.

$\mathcal{L}$ $\mathcal{L}$ $\mathcal{l}$

$\mathcal{L}$ $\mathcal{L}$ $\mathcal{L}$ $\mathcal{L}$

$\mathcal{L}$ $\mathcal{L}$ $\mathcal{L}$ $\mathcal{L}$

$\mathcal{L}$ $\mathcal{L}$ $\mathcal{L}$ $\mathcal{L}$

$\mathcal{L}$ $\mathcal{L}$ $\mathcal{L}$ $\mathcal{L}$

$\mathcal{L}$ $\mathcal{L}$ $\mathcal{L}$ $\mathcal{L}$

$\mathcal{L}$ $\mathcal{L}$ $\mathcal{L}$ $\mathcal{L}$

$\mathcal{l}$ $\mathcal{l}$ $\mathcal{l}$

$\mathcal{l}$ $\mathcal{l}$ $\mathcal{l}$

$\mathcal{l}$ $\mathcal{l}$ $\mathcal{l}$

$\mathcal{l}$ $\mathcal{l}$ $\mathcal{l}$

$\mathcal{l}$ $\mathcal{l}$ $\mathcal{l}$

Trace the letter Mm. Then write the letter Mm as many times as possible.

$\mathcal{M} \ \mathit{m}$

$\mathcal{M} \ \mathcal{M} \ \mathcal{M}$

$\mathcal{M} \ \mathcal{M} \ \mathcal{M}$

$\mathcal{M} \ \mathcal{M} \ \mathcal{M}$

$\mathcal{M} \ \mathcal{M} \ \mathcal{M}$

$\mathcal{M} \ \mathcal{M} \ \mathcal{M}$

$\mathcal{M} \ \mathcal{M} \ \mathcal{M}$

$m \ m \ m$

$m \ m \ m$

$m \ m \ m$

$m \ m \ m$

$m \ m \ m$

Trace the letter Nn. Then write the letter Nn as many times as possible.

𝑛 𝑛

𝑛 𝑛 𝑛

𝑛 𝑛 𝑛

𝑛 𝑛 𝑛

𝑛 𝑛 𝑛

𝑛 𝑛 𝑛

𝑛 𝑛 𝑛

𝑛 𝑛 𝑛

𝑛 𝑛 𝑛

𝑛 𝑛 𝑛

𝑛 𝑛 𝑛

𝑛 𝑛 𝑛

Trace the letter Oo. Then write the letter Oo as many times as possible.

Learn to Write in Cursive: Joining Cursive Letters

Trace the letter Pp. Then write the letter Pp as many times as possible.

Trace the letter Qq. Then write the letter Qq as many times as possible.

$\mathcal{Q}$ q

$\mathcal{Q}$ $\mathcal{Q}$ $\mathcal{Q}$

$\mathcal{Q}$ $\mathcal{Q}$ $\mathcal{Q}$

$\mathcal{Q}$ $\mathcal{Q}$ $\mathcal{Q}$

$\mathcal{Q}$ $\mathcal{Q}$ $\mathcal{Q}$

$\mathcal{Q}$ $\mathcal{Q}$ $\mathcal{Q}$

$\mathcal{Q}$ $\mathcal{Q}$ $\mathcal{Q}$

q q q

q q q

q q q

q q q

q q q

Learn to Write in Cursive: Joining Cursive Letters

Trace the letter Rr. Then write the letter Rr as many times as possible.

Trace the letter Ss. Then write the letter Ss as many times as possible.

Learn to Write in Cursive: Joining Cursive Letters

Trace the letter Tt. Then write the letter Tt as many times as possible.

$\mathcal{T}$ t

$\mathcal{F}$ $\mathcal{F}$ $\mathcal{F}$

$\mathcal{F}$ $\mathcal{F}$ $\mathcal{F}$

$\mathcal{F}$ $\mathcal{F}$ $\mathcal{F}$

$\mathcal{F}$ $\mathcal{F}$ $\mathcal{F}$

$\mathcal{F}$ $\mathcal{F}$ $\mathcal{F}$

$\mathcal{F}$ $\mathcal{F}$ $\mathcal{F}$

t t t

t t t

t t t

t t t

t t t

Trace the letter Uu. Then write the letter Uu as many times as possible.

$\mathcal{U}\ \mathcal{u}$

$\mathcal{U}\quad\mathcal{U}\quad\mathcal{U}$

$\mathcal{U}\quad\mathcal{U}\quad\mathcal{U}$

$\mathcal{U}\quad\mathcal{U}\quad\mathcal{U}$

$\mathcal{U}\quad\mathcal{U}\quad\mathcal{U}$

$\mathcal{U}\quad\mathcal{U}\quad\mathcal{U}$

$\mathcal{U}\quad\mathcal{U}\quad\mathcal{U}$

$\mathcal{u}\quad\mathcal{u}\quad\mathcal{u}$

$\mathcal{u}\quad\mathcal{u}\quad\mathcal{u}$

$\mathcal{u}\quad\mathcal{u}\quad\mathcal{u}$

$\mathcal{u}\quad\mathcal{u}\quad\mathcal{u}$

$\mathcal{u}\quad\mathcal{u}\quad\mathcal{u}$

Learn to Write in Cursive: Joining Cursive Letters

Trace the letter Vv. Then write the letter Vv as many times as possible.

Trace the letter Ww. Then write the letter Ww as many times as possible.

Learn to Write in Cursive: Joining Cursive Letters

Trace the letter Xx. Then write the letter Xx as many times as possible.

$\mathcal{X}$ $\mathcal{x}$

$\mathcal{X}$ $\mathcal{X}$ $\mathcal{X}$

$\mathcal{X}$ $\mathcal{X}$ $\mathcal{X}$

$\mathcal{X}$ $\mathcal{X}$ $\mathcal{X}$

$\mathcal{X}$ $\mathcal{X}$ $\mathcal{X}$

$\mathcal{X}$ $\mathcal{X}$ $\mathcal{X}$

$\mathcal{X}$ $\mathcal{X}$ $\mathcal{X}$

$\mathcal{x}$ $\mathcal{x}$ $\mathcal{x}$

$\mathcal{x}$ $\mathcal{x}$ $\mathcal{x}$

$\mathcal{x}$ $\mathcal{x}$ $\mathcal{x}$

$\mathcal{x}$ $\mathcal{x}$ $\mathcal{x}$

$\mathcal{x}$ $\mathcal{x}$ $\mathcal{x}$

Trace the letter Yy. Then write the letter Yy as many times as possible.

$\mathcal{Y}\ y$

Learn to Write in Cursive: Joining Cursive Letters

Trace the letter Zz. Then write the letter Zz as many times as possible.

UNITED STATES OF AMERICA
States & Capitals

Trace the individual letters. Then trace the joined letters and write the word.

Montgomery

Alabama

Montgomery, Alabama

Alaska

Juneau

Juneau, Alaska

Arizona

Phoenix

Phoenix, Arizona

Learn to Write in Cursive: Joining Cursive Letters

Trace the individual letters. Then trace the joined letters and write the word.

Arkansas

Little Rock

Little Rock, Arkansas

California

Sacramento

Sacramento, California

Colorado

Denver

Denver, Colorado

Trace the individual letters. Then trace the joined letters and write the word.

Connecticut

Hartford

Hartford, Connecticut

Delaware

Dover

Dover, Delaware

Florida

Tallahassee

Tallahassee, Florida

Learn to Write in Cursive: Joining Cursive Letters

Trace the individual letters. Then trace the joined letters and write the word.

Georgia

Atlanta

Atlanta, Georgia

Hawaii

Honolulu

Honolulu, Hawaii

Idaho

Boise

Boise, Idaho

Trace the individual letters. Then trace the joined letters and write the word.

Alabama

Montgomery

Montgomery, Alabama

Illinois

Springfield

Springfield, Illinois

Indiana

Indianapolis

Indianapolis, Indiana

Trace the individual letters. Then trace the joined letters and write the word.

Iowa

Des Moines

Des Moines, Iowa

Kansas

Topeka

Topeka, Kansas

Kentucky

Frankfort

Frankfort, Kentucky

Trace the individual letters. Then trace the joined letters and write the word.

Louisiana

Baton Rouge

Baton Rouge, Louisiana

Maine

Augusta

Augusta, Maine

Maryland

Annapolis

Annapolis, Maryland

Trace the individual letters. Then trace the joined letters and write the word.

Massachusetts

Boston

Boston, Massachusetts

Michigan

Lansing

Lansing, Michigan

Minnesota

St. Paul

St. Paul, Minnesota

Trace the individual letters. Then trace the joined letters and write the word.

Mississippi

Jackson

Jackson, Mississippi

Missouri

Jefferson City

Jefferson City, Missouri

Montana

Helena

Helena, Montana

Learn to Write in Cursive: Joining Cursive Letters

Trace the individual letters. Then trace the joined letters and write the word.

Nebraska

Lincoln

Lincoln, Nebraska

Nevada

Carson City

Carson City, Nevada

New Hampshire

Concord

Concord, New Hampshire

Trace the individual letters. Then trace the joined letters and write the word.

New Jersey

Trenton

Trenton, New Jersey

New Mexico

Santa Fe

Santa Fe, New Mexico

New York

Albany

Albany, New York

Learn to Write in Cursive: Joining Cursive Letters

Trace the individual letters. Then trace the joined letters and write the word.

North Carolina

Raleigh

Raleigh, North Carolina

North Dakota

Bismarck

Bismarck, North Dakota

Ohio

Columbus

Columbus, Ohio

Trace the individual letters. Then trace the joined letters and write the word.

Oklahoma

Oklahoma City

Oklahoma City, Oklahoma

Oregon

Salem

Salem, Oregon

Pennsylvania

Harrisburg

Harrisburg, Pennsylvania

Learn to Write in Cursive: Joining Cursive Letters

Trace the individual letters. Then trace the joined letters and write the word.

Rhode Island

Providence

Providence, Rhode Island

South Carolina

Columbia

Columbia, South Carolina

South Dakota

Pierre

Pierre, South Dakota

Trace the individual letters. Then trace the joined letters and write the word.

Tennessee

Nashville

Nashville, Tennessee

Texas

Austin

Austin, Texas

Utah

Salt Lake City

Salt Lake City, Utah

Learn to Write in Cursive: Joining Cursive Letters

Trace the individual letters. Then trace the joined letters and write the word.

Vermont

Montpelier

Montpelier, Vermont

Washington

Olympia

Olympia, Washington

West Virginia

Charleston

Charleston, West Virginia

Trace the individual letters. Then trace the joined letters and write the word.

Wisconsin

Madison

Madison, Wisconsin

Wyoming

Cheyenne

Cheyenne, Wyoming

United States of

America

United States of America

UNITED STATES
Presidents

Trace the individual letters. Then trace the joined letters and write the word.

George

Washington

George Washington

John

Adams

John Adams

Thomas

Jefferson

Thomas Jefferson

Learn to Write in Cursive: Joining Cursive Letters

Trace the individual letters. Then trace the joined letters and write the word.

James

Madison

James Madison

James

Monroe

James Monroe

John Quincy

Adams

John Quincy Adams

Trace the individual letters. Then trace the joined letters and write the word.

Andrew

Jackson

Andrew Jackson

Martin

Van Buren

Martin Van Buren

William Henry

Harrison

William Henry Harrison

Learn to Write in Cursive: Joining Cursive Letters

Trace the individual letters. Then trace the joined letters and write the word.

John

Tyler

John Tyler

James K.

Polk

James K. Polk

Zachary

Taylor

Zachary Taylor

Trace the individual letters. Then trace the joined letters and write the word.

Millard

Fillmore

Millard Fillmore

Franklin

Pierce

Franklin Pierce

James

Buchanan

James Buchanan

Learn to Write in Cursive: Joining Cursive Letters

Trace the individual letters. Then trace the joined letters and write the word.

Abraham

Lincoln

Abraham Lincoln

Andrew

Johnson

Andrew Johnson

Ulysses S.

Grant

Ulysses S. Grant

Trace the individual letters. Then trace the joined letters and write the word.

Rutherford B.

Hayes

Rutherford B. Hayes

James A.

Garfield

James A. Garfield

Chester A.

Arthur

Chester A. Arthur

Trace the individual letters. Then trace the joined letters and write the word.

Grover

Cleveland

Grover Cleveland (1st term)

Benjamin

Harrison

Benjamin Harrison

Grover

Cleveland

Grover Cleveland (2nd term)

Trace the individual letters. Then trace the joined letters and write the word.

William

McKinley

William McKinley

Theodore

Roosevelt

Theodore Roosevelt

William H.

Taft

William H. Taft

Learn to Write in Cursive: Joining Cursive Letters

Trace the individual letters. Then trace the joined letters and write the word.

Woodrow

Wilson

Woodrow Wilson

Warren G.

Harding

Warren G. Harding

Calvin

Coolidge

Calvin Coolidge

Trace the individual letters. Then trace the joined letters and write the word.

Herbert

Hoover

Herbert Hoover

Franklin D.

Roosevelt

Franklin D. Roosevelt

Harry S.

Truman

Harry S. Truman

Learn to Write in Cursive: Joining Cursive Letters

Trace the individual letters. Then trace the joined letters and write the word.

Dwight D.

Eisenhower

Dwight D. Eisenhower

John F.

Kennedy

John F. Kennedy

Lyndon B.

Johnson

Lyndon B. Johnson

Trace the individual letters. Then trace the joined letters and write the word.

Richard M.

Nixon

Richard M. Nixon

Gerald R.

Ford

Gerald R. Ford

Jimmy

Carter

Jimmy Carter

Trace the individual letters. Then trace the joined letters and write the word.

Ronald

Reagan

Ronald Reagan

George

Bush

George Bush

William "Bill"

Clinton

William "Bill" Clinton

Trace the individual letters. Then trace the joined letters and write the word.

George W.

Bush

George W. Bush

Barack

Obama

Barack Obama

United States

Presidents

United States Presidents

Learn to Write in Cursive: Joining Cursive Letters

Made in the USA
Las Vegas, NV
04 April 2024